Faro
Travel Guide

*Sightseeing, Hotel, Restaurant
& Shopping Highlights*

Jessica Doherty

Table of Contents

Faro

Mainland Portugal's southernmost city, scenic Faro is the capital of the Algarve. A colourful town marked by long sandy beaches and flanked by dramatic rocks. Born inside medieval walls, the city unfolds its long story; one of a mish-mash of influences and periods of both prominence and devastation.

Unfortunately, most foreign sun-seekers are often whisked away to other parts of the region shortly upon arrival to Faro, with the town of 50,000 inhabitants serving as a main gateway to the wider Algarve area. By doing so, they are overlooking the surprising beauty that is Faro – endless sweeping beaches, a historic old town and a delightful National Park all on its doorstep, waiting to be explored.

The scenery in Faro is unlike what one finds elsewhere in Algarve, where steep cliffs, majestic rocks and wild waves dominate the landscape. Here, tranquil waters and white sands are the ruling elements, making Faro a particularly good bet for family beach vacations.

Step away from the sand and you will find yourself wandering around the charming and compact old town. Lose yourself in the pedestrianized meandering streets paved with lovely mosaics and don't forget to take every chance you get to catch breath-taking views towards Faro's harbor. The historic center is endlessly alluring with its period architecture, landmark arches and the magnificent cathedral. What survives here stands as a proud and characterful testament to an oft-painful history, one marked by war tragedies and natural catastrophes.

The lagoon of Ria Formosa has been inhabited since the Paleolithic age. During the Roman occupation period, a settlement by the name of Ossonoba stood on the location of today's Faro and rose to importance due to its port, fishing and salt industry. A Moorish rule in the 8th century made Ossonoba a vital commercial town, with it briefly becoming a princedom capital in the 9th century.

It was around this time that a different name began being used for the town; called Santa Maria during the period, it later became known as Harun, which gave it its current name. The Moors left a profound mark in Faro's history up until their defeat by the Portuguese King Afonso III during the Reconquista in 1249, when the city became Algarve's most prominent one.

Sacked by the Earl of Essex in 1596 and reduced to shambles, it became secondary to Lagos which had already imposed itself as a capital. This lasted until the historic 1755 earthquake that heavily damaged most coastal towns with the exception of Faro. Although impacted as well, the town was protected by the sandy coast of the Ria Formosa lagoon and its superior sheltered position has lent it the administrative powers it still enjoys today.

Although chances are you will be tantalized enough by Faro to be content to stay here for the full course of your vacation, nearby attractions are sure to beckon you with their proximity and significance. Due to its location in the center of Algarve, Faro is a great base for those wanting to explore the wider region. Tour the magnificent beaches sprinkled around the Ria Formosa Nature Park, explore the ruins in close by Estoi and don't miss a chance to see the yachting lifestyle in the exclusive Vilamoura marina. Whatever you are looking for from your holiday, Faro is sure to deliver.

Culture

The last town on the Iberian Peninsula to be liberated from Islamic rule, Faro's culture is invariably influenced by the diversity of peoples that have inhabited the area during its long history. A notable Moorish stamp is evident in landmarks and the general architecture of white-washed houses, with a certain feeling of an old world culture hard to brush off as you wander the maze of alleys in the center.

To begin to understand some of the history that sets the backbone to Faro's culture, pay attention to the ceramic tiles (*azulejos*) around the old town, which depict historic scenes and provide insight into the complexities of the town's past. Here, Baroque, Gothic and Renaissance styles converge into an architectural fusion, mirrored by the history of the city's most important landmarks; Faro's Cathedral, for example, has previously served as a Roman forum and subsequently a mosque.

For an in-depth coverage of the region's cultural heritage, check out the Municipal Museum chock-full of local ancient artifacts. Nearby Estoi with its Milreu Ruins is a magnet for history buffs where you can find one of the world's oldest churches. Additionally, whiffs of ancient Roman civilizations await you in the Cerro da Vila ruins in nearby Vilamoura.

If you are planning to travel to Faro during August, your visit may coincide with the annual FolkFaro festival (www.folkfaro.com) which takes place August 17-25. The festival is a colorful celebration of the region's folklore, but is also decidedly international, with performers, parades and various shows with worldwide participants.

Location & Orientation

The reason why Faro is a popular entry point for Algarve visitors is the proximity of the airport. At only 5 kilometers away from the city, Faro's airport (FAO) has witnessed a consistent increase of number of travelers, with low-cost airlines flocking to it in recent years.

Connected to the city center by bus and taxi, the airport is a mere 20-minute ride away (€2.20 by bus or about €10 by taxi)

Other options for arrival into Faro include a high-speed train from Lisbon (a 2.5 hour ride) as well as regional trains which connect it to other points along the Algarve coast.

Those wanting to discover the wider region should consider visiting with a vehicle (or hiring one), which will also enable you to explore at will. That being said, bus lines between Faro and a number of other cities on the Iberian Peninsula (including Lisbon, Porto, Madrid and Seville) run daily.

While walking within Faro is an enjoyable way to see the city, consider packing adequate footwear to avoid uncomfortable strolls around the cobblestone streets. If you are planning to use the public transportation within Faro, you should be looking out for buses number 14 and 16, which circulate around the city and travel as far as the airport and the Faro beach. Tickets can be bought on board and cost €2.20.

Climate & When to Visit

A moderate Mediterranean climate, plenty of sunshine and a perpetual breeze make Faro a favorite destination year-round, with the Algarve winter being far from the gray and gloomy scenery found in European vacation spots further north.

Sunny days and temperatures averaging between 12 (54 °F) and 16 C (61 °F) are the norm here during winter, though you should be prepared for frequent rain if you choose to visit Faro in the off-season.

Considered one of Europe's sunniest places, Faro's temperatures are pleasant throughout the year. But perhaps the best time to visit it is at very earliest of summer, when the air is still fresh but the sea is comfortably warm for a swim. Be prepared for a few colder nights up until June, and pack a change of warmer clothes just to be sure.

A lot of visitors prefer the months of July and August which can be considerably warmer and significantly busier. Average daily temperatures range between 27 and 35 °C (81–95 °F). But regardless of how hot it gets, the pleasant sea breezes are sure to help you keep your cool. The warm weather stretches well into fall, with October temperatures sometimes even approaching 30 C (85 °F).

Money & Currency

The official currency in Portugal is the Euro. Prices encountered during your Faro holiday will vary depending on your choice of accommodation, entertainment and itinerary plans. However, as Faro is a working city and is often overlooked by tourists, prices here are generally more affordable than in other resorts around the Algarve. In fact, it has been voted as one of the most affordable European beach destinations, with fantastic value accommodation and eating options.

Maps

For an excellent and comprehensive map of Faro city centre, see:
http://www.farouncovered.com/Portals/Faro/map/map_faro.pdf

Sightseeing Highlights

Old Town

The so-called Cidade Velha, Faro's old town, is a well-preserved historic section just to the east of the harbor. Winding cobblestone streets, Moorish-inspired architecture and a definitive sense of traveling back in time will make you want to wander around the 9th-century town for hours on end, marveling the lively mix of styles that has added multiple layers to Faro's character. Tragically, the historic center was burned down by the English troops in 1596 and then rebuilt only to be destroyed once again in the 1755 earthquake.

Remains surviving the Reconquista as well as the devastating earthquake today compete with 19th-century architecture in this delightful maze of alleys. Enter the city thought the significant 18th-century Arco de Villa arch and head towards the Faro Cathedral (Sé) on the orange tree-lined square. The nearby 18th-century Bishop's Palace is a good landmark to walk by before heading to the Municipal Museum where archeological relics unveil the city's long and eventful history.

To exit the historic center, go through the Arco da Porta Nova, a place where the old town meets the water and a departure point for boats heading to the Ria Formosa Natural Park.

Arco de Vila

An 18th-century gateway marking the entrance to the Cidade Velha, the Arco de Vila (Arch of the City) is a neoclassical arch built by the order of the Bishop Francisco Gomes. Designed by Francisco Xavier Fabri and constructed in 1812, the Arco de Vila sits on the site of a former medieval castle gate. With a Moorish portico and a strong brick-vaulted roof, the arch supports the statue of St. Thomas Aquinas (patron saint of Faro). Just above the gateway is the bell tower.

Walk towards the Largo da Sé Street opening up from the gate and you will soon catch a sign of the famous Sé Cathedral as well as the Bishop's Palace – two more landmarks closely most frequently associated with the city.

Cathedral

Largo da Sé, Faro
Tel: +351 289 806 632

Known simply as "Sé" among locals, the 13th-century Faro Cathedral dominates the old town district and is the area's crown jewel. Constructed on the site of a Roman forum turned into a Visigoth cathedral and later into a mosque, the Cathedral was completed in 1251 and its original exterior was clearly Romanesque-Gothic.

Largely rebuilt and renovated after the 1755 earthquake, its tower gate remains an original, as do several chapels. The renovation has resulted in a particularly varied mix of styles, including Baroque, Renaissance and Gothic, perfectly mirroring the city's eclectic collection of period architecture. And though its exterior may not be earth-shattering, the interior definitely is worth a peek; elaborate tiles and gilded carvings as well as a baroque organ are just some of the treasures found on the inside.

If you are on the hunt for spectacular views, make the effort to climb up to the rooftop lookout (*miradouro*) where you also may catch a glimpse of the storks that have made home in the bell towers. From here, you can get a bird's eye view of the typical Portuguese architecture present in Faro, including the iconic red rooftops called *tesouro* as well as the Ria Formosa Park with its magnificent lagoon.

The Cathedral is open daily from 09:00 to 12:30 and from 13:30 to 17:00 while Sunday mass is held at 10:00 and 12:00.

Admission costs €3. Entrance to the cathedral's gilded altar as well as the marbled tombs and chapels costs additional €3.

Bishop's Palace

Largo da Sé 15, Faro

Just opposite the Cathedral is the Bishop's Palace (Paco Episcopal), decorated in multicolored 18-th century hand-painted tiles (*azulejos*). With its red roof, it nowadays is a venue for various religious art exhibitions while its interior is a piece of art itself. The Palace was constructed at the site of the previous Episcopal residence, which was destroyed by the British troops in 1596. Rebuilt after the earthquake, its altarpiece was created in 1786.

Being still the official residence of the Bishop of Faro, the Palace is not open to the public but is nevertheless a lovely landmark to walk by. If your visit coincides with one of the occasional temporary exhibitions held here, you should use the opportunity to take a peek inside.

Municipal Museum of Archeology

Largo Dom Afonso III, Faro
Tel: +351 289 897 400

Housed in one of Portugal's oldest convents – the 16th-century *Convento de Nossa Senhora da Assuncao* - the Municipal Museum of Archeology is one of Algarve's first museums. The museum surveys two millennia's worth of local history and art and is the proud home of the majestic Roman *Mosaic of the Ocean*, depicting Neptune and the Four Winds. Dating to the 3rd century, the mosaic was discovered in 1976 on a building site. A lovely cloister as well as other Roman and Moorish artifacts (both archeological and ecclesiastical) can also be found inside, including many relics excavated at the nearby Estoi site. The famous Faro-born painter Carlos Filipe Porfirio is represented with his moody paintings featuring local legends and religious motifs.

The Museum is open from 09:30 to 17:30 (from 11:30 on weekends) in the summer season and from 10:00 to 18:00 (from 14:00 on weekends) between the months of October and April. Admission fee costs €3 (€1.50 for students).

Ria Formosa Nature Park

Spanning about 60 kilometers of south Portugal's coastline, the Ria Formosa Natural Par was declared one of the country's great natural wonders and is an area of major ecological interest.

A lagoon formed by a sequence of sandpits (*Ilhas*) is the home of wetlands and has been protected since 1987. Unique natural conditions make it a breeding spot for birds, some of which are extremely rare, as well as a variety of marine life. At peak times in the winter season during migration, the park often hosts as many as 20,000 birds, with resident flamingos and the Purple Swamphen being the most recognizable species. A salt production site during Roman times, the landscape of the lagoon changes as one season gives way to the next, with parts of the park sometimes submerged and other times entirely exposed. Today, the area is used for oyster and mussel farming, mostly with the utilization of traditional methods in order to preserve the habitat.

Two peninsulas (Ancao and Cacela) as well as five islands (Barreta, Culatra, Armona, Tavira and Cabanas) make up the Ria Formosa Park. Accessible by small boats from the historic center, the Park can be visited as part of a two and a half hour boat trip (including a 40 minute stay on one of the islands), with prices starting from €10. Full day tours are also available and cost anywhere from €30 to €50 per adult, depending on the tour operator.

Our Lady of Carmel Church & Chapel of Bones

Largo do Carmo, Faro
Tel: +351 289 824 490

Back to the mainland from the Ria Formosa Park and right at the exit of the old town, continue your Faro exploration by moving slightly inland. Just away from the town wall you will soon discover the baroque Igreja de Nossa Senhora do Carmo (Our Lady of Carmel Church). Started in 1713 and completed in 1719 during Joao V's rule, with its façade finished after the historic 1755 earthquake, this Carmelite church is extensively gilded with Brazilian gold in its interior and features imposing twin towers. It also contains significant religious statues, including the nine Triumphal Procession statues by Manuel Martins who also created the Santa Teresa altarpiece.

For those looking for something completely unusual and borderline bizarre, the 19th century Capela dos Ossos (Chapel of Bones) is a true find. The chapel is literally built from and decorated with the bones and skulls of 1,200 monks, all neatly arranged in rows. Completed in 1816, it is a peculiar work of art of the Carmelite monks who built it, inclined to use the remains of their predecessors from a nearby cemetery as a grim reminder of mortality. Entrance fee to this ghoulish chapel costs €1.

Beaches

When you acquainted yourself with Faro's history and culture, the logical choice is to head to one (or more) of the nearby exquisite beaches. Most of the beaches in and around Faro are located on the shallow pits of sand that run along the coastline. This natural landscape creates a wetland lagoon on the internal side, marked by calm and clear waters. The external, ocean-meeting side is somewhat wilder, with waves rolling in from the Atlantic.

Praia de Faro & Ilha de Faro

Faro's beach is a long, gently-sloping stretch of golden sand on Ilha de Faro (Faro Island), some 10 kilometers away from the city. Located on the sandbar that wraps around the coastline, it gets a bit crowded in July and August but nevertheless manages to please all tastes; with gorgeous views, a multitude of facilities and a wide range of entertainment options, it is truly the locals' favorite hangout in the summertime.

To get to the beach, take bus 14 or 16 from across the bus station in the city. The buses run about once every 30 minutes in the summertime and make a stop at the airport. The 45-minute journey itself is irresistibly scenic, particularly when crossing the pine forest region.

Ilha de Barreta/Deserta

Catch a ferry to Ilha de Barreta (also known as Ilha Deserta) to marvel at the long and narrow strip of sand just off the mainland and part of the Ria Formosa National Park. The sandpit that curves around the coast just in front of Faro can be accessed from various points on the mainland. The mind-blowing 10 kilometers of sweeping sands are connected to the wetlands where exotic flamingoes thrive so they provide a different experience from the one usually found on urban purposefully-organized beaches.

Ilha de Barreta is particularly well suited to explorers, with plenty of nature trails available for a change of pace from the more common beach activities. Note that only one restaurant serves the beach, so bringing a snack is recommended.

Vale de Lobo

If you head west of Faro, you will run into the popular Vale do Lobo resort whose dramatic Algarve-typical cliffs provide a stunning change of scenery. A wide beach awaits sun-worshipers, ready to provide its excellent facilities, cafes, bars and restaurants. Vale de Lobo's square (known as Praca) can be found right on the beach while those looking to explore further can head to the golf resort nearby.

Armona

One of the region's most popular beaches, Armona is located east of Faro about 2 kilometers off the Olhao coast and is accessible via ferry from Olhao or Fuseta. Endless sand stretches as far as the eye can reach, inviting leisurely strolls by the water's edge. The sand dunes in the background are home to a number of restaurants and bars while a camping site can also be found nearby.

Living Science Centre

Centro de Ciência Viva, Rua Comandante Francisco Manuel, Faro
Tel: +351 289 890 920
http://www.ccvalg.pt

Faro's Living Science Centre is a great way to spend a day away from the beach, particularly for families with children. A place of learning and discovery, it features interactive exhibitions covering a multitude of areas, such as light, the solar system, and the human body, among others. Children's curious minds will have a chance to look at planets through a telescope or discover marine life with the use of microscopes. Permanent exhibitions dedicated to the sea as well as a flight simulator and astronomical observation sessions are just a few more of the many activities the whole family can engage in during the visit. Opened since 1997, the Living Science Centre is housed in the old fire station near the Manuel Bivar gardens. Entrance costs €3.50 for adults; €1.75 for children under 12.

Estoi & the Milreu Ruins

Just 11 kilometers north of Faro and set in the gorgeous countryside, Estoi is a quaint old town that easily justifies a half-day trip. A bus connects Faro and Estoi and drops visitors off in the main square, close to the 18th century pink rococo Palacio do Visconde de Estoi, nowadays a private palace. The Palace also features beautiful shaded gardens with tropic plants, open to the public.

Stroll downhill from the main square towards the 1st century Milreu Roman site and you will soon find the most compelling reason to visit Estoi - a locality that used to be inhabited between the 2nd and the 10th century, this is Algarve's most impressive and expansive Roman ruins site. Built in the style of a peristyle villa (a columned porch surrounding a court), it features intact columns and original mosaics. A temple originally devoted to the cult of water, then converted to a basilica in the 3rd century AD, is one of the world's oldest churches. The remains of a bathing complex have also withheld the test of time, and feature fish mosaics in the bathrooms and an intricate changing room including a *frigidarium* designed to hold cold water. The villa used to feature an advanced water supply network as well as heated rooms and thermal springs.

Check out the amusing decorations found around the ruins, with fish represented as particularly fat in order to create the optical illusion of movement, testifying to the level of dedication to detail and effort put into the creation of this ancient villa.

Entrance into the ruins costs €2 and they are open from 10:30 to 13:00 and from 14:00 to 18:30 daily between May and September; 09:30 to 13:00 and 14:00 to 17:00 the rest of the year.

Tavira

Another popular day trip out of Faro is Tavira, one of Algarve's prettiest towns. Only 30 kilometers east of Faro and sitting on both sides of the Gilao River, this traditional fishing town was founded as early as 4th century BC and served as a port for trading with North Africa. Tavira is a popular destination not only for its picturesque beauty defined by graceful 18th-century houses, palm trees and low bridges, but also because of the spectacular beach on Ilha de Tavira.

Roman Bridge

Today's bridge being mostly built in 1667 on top of a previous structure, the Roman Bridge was initially constructed during the Islamic al-Andalus rule in Tavira. A vital factor in the defense system of medieval Tavira, it used to have houses erected on it as it connected the two banks of the River Gilao. Collapsing in 1655, it was rebuilt about a decade later, largely featuring today's characteristics.

Partially destroyed once again in the 1989 flood but quickly restored, it is no longer used for motor vehicle traffic and is fully pedestrianized, thus inviting a leisurely stroll.

An interesting detail worth noting is the fact that the river to the west of the bridge is known as Gilao while the very same river goes by the name Sequa to east; the reason can be found in a complex local legend that involves two lovers who had tragically drowned on either side of the bridge.

Tavira Island

Easily accessible from the town of Tavira via a ferry, the Ilha de Tavira (Tavira Island) stretches out towards the southwest and is a giant 14-kilometers-long beach with spectacular dunes in the background. Its width varies between 150 meters and 1 kilometer, making it seem truly endless at times. Likely one of Algarve's best beaches, it is typically flocked to in the summertime but it is relatively easy to steer clear of the crowds on such a large stretch. Even naturists can find spots specifically designed for them on Ilha de Tavira. Bars and restaurants cater to travelers' every needs as does the variety of beach sceneries – those looking for more tranquil waters should head to the lagoon-facing side, while those not intimidated by waves will delight if they choose the Atlantic-facing orientation.

Tavira's blue flag beach can be accessed from the mainland (Quatro Aguas) via frequent ferries (from €1.50 round trip) or water taxis (from €20). If you are charmed by the beach and wish to spend a night on Tavira Island, look into the camping site under the pine trees – the only available overnight accommodation on the Ilha de Tavira.

Vilamoura

Vilamoura is a luxurious tourist resort and the largest complex of its kind in Europe. Stretching over an area of 20 km², it was built with a purpose to accommodate a variety of tastes and is most notably known for its marina, golf course complexes and a dense population of hotels. For those looking for a bit of history and culture, the nearby Cerro da Vila ruins are a logical choice as they are one of the most significant archeological sites in the country.

Vilamoura is located 23 kilometers west of Faro and is accessible via bus (€4 one way) or taxi (starting from €27 one way).

Vilamoura Marina

Vilamoura
Tel: +351 289 310 560
http://www.marinadevilamoura.com/en

The main center of activity in Vilamoura, the marina is alive with restaurants, bars and shops, some of which are decidedly upscale. This is Portugal's largest marina and is sure to keep you entertained for hours. Peaceful during the day and pulsing with life at night, it attracts everyday folk as well as the wealthy and the popular.

With a capacity to berth more than 1,000 boats, it sees a lot of yacht traffic and also provides options for chartering boats.

Water sports activities are frequently organized as well, and include deep-sea fishing, cruises and scuba diving. The marina was recently voted Best Portuguese Marina for 2013 and certainly makes Vilamoura a particularly cosmopolitan destination along the Algarve coast.

Cerro da Vila

Avenida Cerro Da Vila, 8125-403 Vilamoura
Tel: +351 289 312 153

Just steps from the marina, the Cerro da Vila ruins with leftovers from ancient civilizations are a great way to spend a few more hours in Vilamoura. The particular site has been occupied since the Bronze Age but the earliest settlers were the Romans who have left an unmistakable mark on the area, mostly between the 2nd and 3rd century AD. Cerro da Vila then belonged to the Ossonoba province and served the lands around the settlement with its port.

Remnants of a rustic mansion (Roman Villa), public bath-houses and fish salting tanks can be found on this ruins complex, as well as foundations of a tower used for burials. The area is nowadays an archeological site of immense importance in Algarve. A museum has been created within the complex, to serve as a guide to visitors wanting to further explore the significance of the site. The ruins are open from 10:00 to 13:00 and from 16:00 to 21:00 in the summertime. Between the months of November and April you can visit the Cerro da Villa from 09:30 to 12:30 or from 14:00 to 18:00. Entrance to the site costs €5.

Recommendations for the Budget Traveller

Places To Stay

Casa d'Alagoa Hostel

Praca Alexandre Herculano 27, 8000-160 Faro
Tel: +351 289 813 252
http://farohostel.com/

If you don't mind staying in a hostel, consider the historical Casa d'Alagoa – an affordable accommodation in central Faro that is sure to please a range of tastes.

Both private and shared rooms are available in this excellently located and clean hostel just across the Alagoa garden, with great connections to Faro's beaches. One can also easily reach the historic Arco da Vila in only 5 minutes on foot.

The high-ceilinged rooms come equipped with Wi-Fi, a buffet breakfast and the use of a convenient communal kitchen. Laundry services and bike rentals are also available through the staff reception desk.

At the start of the summer season, private bathroom double rooms start from €48 per night, including breakfast while beds in shared dormitories start from €17 per night.

Hotel Ibis Faro

Estrada Nacional 125, 8000-770 Faro
Tel: +351 289 893 800
http://www.ibis.com/gb/hotel-1593-ibis-faro/index.shtml

Just two kilometers from Faro's center, the Hotel Ibis Faro – part of the Ibis chain of hotels – is perfectly located for easy access to the nearby beaches, the Ria Formosa Natural Park and the historic center with its landmarks. The hotel's 81 rooms all include Wi-Fi access and are simply decorated, with private bathrooms and A/C. An outdoor swimming pool and a bar with a terrace are available for hotel's guests as is the private parking. Golf lovers should know that the nearest course is merely 10 kilometers away.

Double rooms in the early summer season (June) start from €49 per night, with an optional breakfast price of €6 per person per night.

Hotel Adelaide

Rua Cruz das Mestras n 9, 8000-261 Faro
Tel: +351 289 802
http://www.adelaideresidencial.net

For another affordable option in central Faro, travelers should look into the 2-star Hotel Adelaide – a 19-room hotel within walking distance of the Faro bus station and the marina. Rooms are bright and offer free Wi-Fi and air-conditioning while the hotel also has a restaurant serving daily buffet breakfast. Shared kitchen facilities are also available for use by hotel's guests.

The 19 double rooms in the Adelaide are available at rates starting at €50 per night in the mid-season, breakfast included.

Hotel Faro

Praça D. Francisco Gomes, N 2, 8000 -168 Faro
Tel: +351 289 830 830
http://www.hotelfaro.pt/

If you are looking for affordable accommodation right in the middle of Faro's center, look no further than Hotel Faro, a 4-star choice overlooking the old town and the marina. Large and bright rooms come with cable TV, a minibar and private bathrooms, while some also include balconies. A buffet breakfast is optional and a restaurant on the rooftop serves Portuguese cuisine as well.

Prices for one of Hotel Faro's 90 rooms start from €75 for a double room in the mid-season, breakfast included.

Quinta dos Poetas, Hotel Rural Olhao

Sítio da Arretorta, 8700-180 Olhão
Tel: + 351 289 990 990
http://www.quintadospoetas.com/

Outside Faro and in located in Olhao's countryside, the Hotel Rural Quinta dos Poetas is set against picturesque scenery. Providing 22 rooms with private balconies, air-condition and wooden furniture, the hotel also offers a pool, a fitness room and a local cuisine restaurant.

 Renting a bicycle to explore the nearby Ria Formosa is easy and is a great option for nature lovers. Free private parking is also available on the hotel's grounds.

Double rooms with breakfast in the early summer season start at €75 per night.

Places to Eat & Drink

Columbus Cocktail and Wine Bar

Praca Dom Francisco Gomes, 13, Faro
Tel: +351 917 762 22
http://www.barcolumbus.pt/

Head here right before dinner for a glass of perfect
sangria or for a delicious cocktail afterwards. Columbus
Bar, located just across from the marina, is a favorite with
locals and tourists alike and serves a wide range of
excellent cocktails on a nice terrace.

A stylish bar inside is another option for visitors and the
attentive staff also serves delicious tapas. Cocktails cost
about €6 and some of the more popular ones include the
Strawberry Daiquiri and the Cosmopolitan. The clientele
is varied at this popular bar, with hordes of repeat visitors
coming in from all over Algarve.

Tasca do Ricky

Rua do Forno, N021, Faro
Tel: +351 919 111 057

This typical Portuguese tasca (small restaurant) is a great choice for a filling and affordable lunch, with a large portion main dish, dessert, drink and coffee setting you back a mere €6. Home-cooked food and a very friendly service are Ricky's trademark as the owner is known to personally greet patrons at the door. Don't ask for a menu; simply follow his instructions as he guides you through what is at its best and freshest that day. The restaurant is closed on Sunday evenings.

Jamie's Faro

Largo de Sao Pedro 54, Faro
Tel: +351 961 480 083
http://www.jamiesfaro.com/

Definitely one of the more popular restaurants in the city, Jamie's Faro offers excellent value for money. Located near the Chapel of Bones, it features a lovely terrace providing a relaxed setting for al-fresco dining as well as impeccable service by the courteous staff. The menu of the day costs just under €9 and includes a dish (selected from four options), drink and coffee. Try the risotto with grilled stuffed chicken and the exquisite chocolate mousse and don't skip a glass of the excellent house white wine.

Adega Nova

Rua Francisco Barreto, 24, Faro
Tel: +351 289 813 433

The rustic and informal Adega Nova serves quality food which changes ever so slightly day by day. Try the Algarve cheese as a starter and continue on to sample delightful fresh seafood such as octopus with rice or the mixed seafood skewer (€13). Wash it all down with the young sparkling wine Vinho Verde as you chat with the locals sitting on the next table for a true cultural immersion experience.

Atelier de Comida Sto Antonio

Largo de Camoes 23/24, Faro
Tel: +351 289 802 148
http://www.atelierdecomida.com/

Excellent food and wine await you in the Atelier de Comida Sto Antonio and you will soon realize that the restaurant is packed with locals – always a good sign. The backyard is a lovely setting for outdoor dining in the summertime. Competitively priced and delicious dishes include monkfish shish-kebab (€12.50), sauteed sea bream (€12.50), bacon-wrapped sea bass (€13.50) and pork tenderloin with clams (€11.50), to name just a few. Takeaway options are also available, with the soup of the day particularly well priced at only €1.

Places To Shop

Forum Algarve

Forum Algarve EN 125 Km 103, Faro
Tel: +351 289 889 300
http://www.forumalgarve.net/

The Forum Algarve shopping mall, located on the main EN125 road, has a wide selection of shops, restaurants and cafes and an open air central square. Shopping aficionados will delight at the more than 100 stores spanning a wide range of goods (including fashion, cosmetics, home ware, books, gifts and a good selection of services). There is also a cinema complex in the Forum, a large supermarket as well as over 20 different restaurant and café establishments. The Forum Algarve is easibly accessible by public minibus transport which runs every 15 minutes.

Mercado Municipal de Faro

Largo Doutor Francisco Sá Carneiro, Faro
Tel: +351 289 897 250
http://www.mercadomunicipaldefaro.pt

If you are on the hunt for fresh produce or simply want to mingle with the locals, head to the Mercado Municipal where countless stalls will delight you with the freshest of ingredients and their varied offerings. The indoor market is a heaven for foodies and those looking to stock up on food gifts (such as salty olives and cured meats) all at amazingly low prices. For a sweet treat while you shop, try the delicious custard tarts.

Carminho

Rua Santo António 29, Faro
Tel: +351 289 826 522

Most of Faro's shopping can be found along the Rua Santo Antonio street right in the center of the city. If you have souvenir shopping to do, check out the Carminho store where handicrafts and some traditional Portuguese attire await you. Traditional painted *azulejos*, tableware, embroidery and items made of copper are just a few more of the products on sale at the well-stocked Carminho.

Garrafeira Rui

Praça Ferreira de Almeida, 28, 8000 Faro
Tel: +351 289 822 803

If you have, like many others before you, fallen in love with delicious Portuguese wines, head to the Garrafeira Rui – Faro's best known wine shop. Here you can stock up on local wines and port as well as purchase local delicacies, such as sausages, cheeses and sweets. The store is open Monday to Saturday from 08:00 to 20:00.

Estoi Flea Market

If you can time your visit to Estoi to coincide with the 2nd Sunday of the month, take advantage of the large open air market where traders from all over the region congregate to sell produce, clothing, antiques and a large selection of handmade crafts. Items worth hunting for here include hats and baskets woven from palm leaves – one of Algarve's most popular souvenirs.

Printed in Great Britain
by Amazon